Hey.
These are the thoughts that swirl in my brain.
Some unbidden, echoes of the past.
Others are words of resilience and hope to fight against them.
Color in my doodles. Add in your own words and pictures.
Let's fight our demons together.

delve
dig deep

color away, my darlings

delve into the pain
that's where the healing is

you will ride out this storm
just like all the others

why
are
so
my
fucking
thoughts
tangled

why does it feel like my brain is on fire

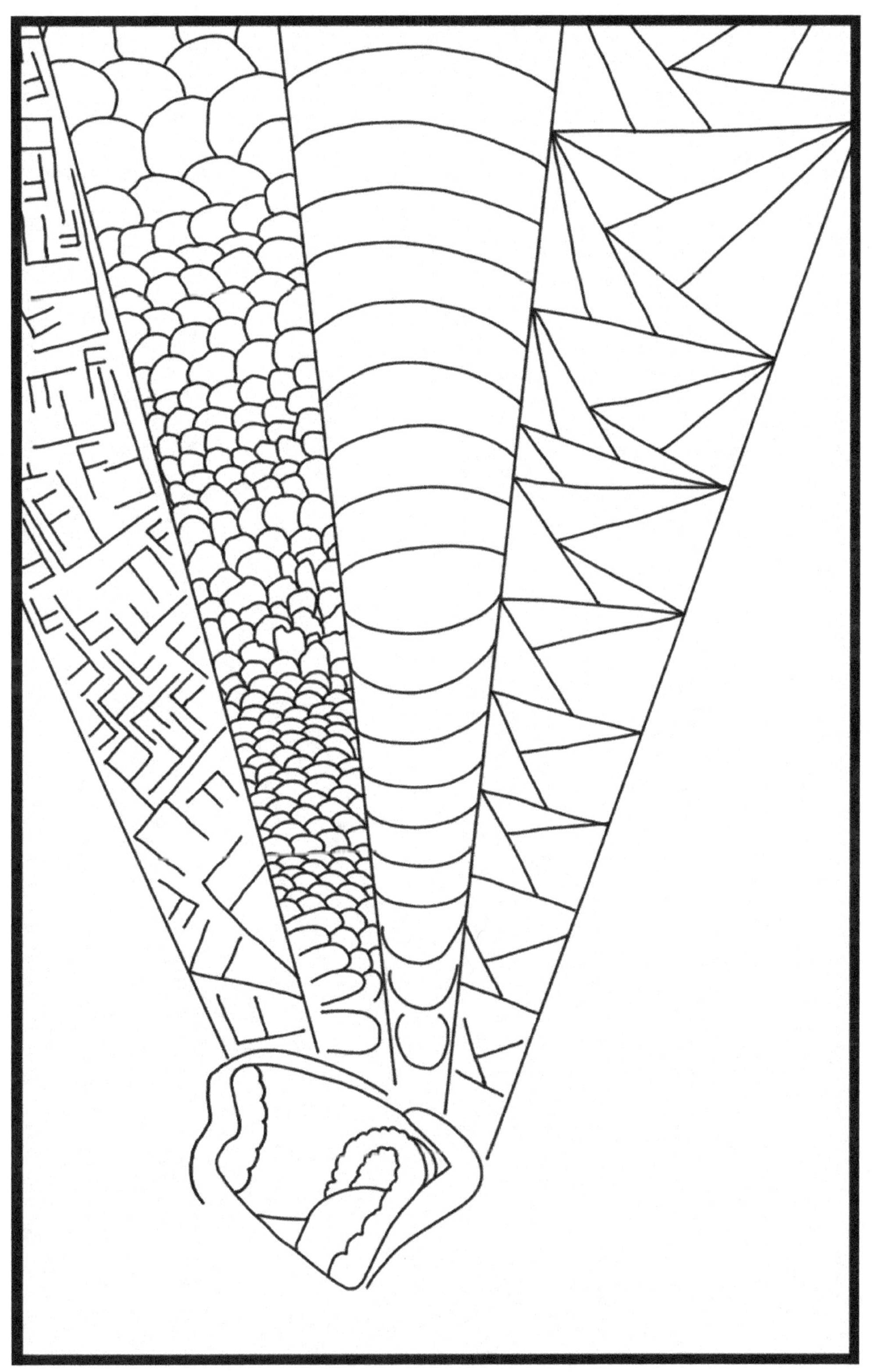

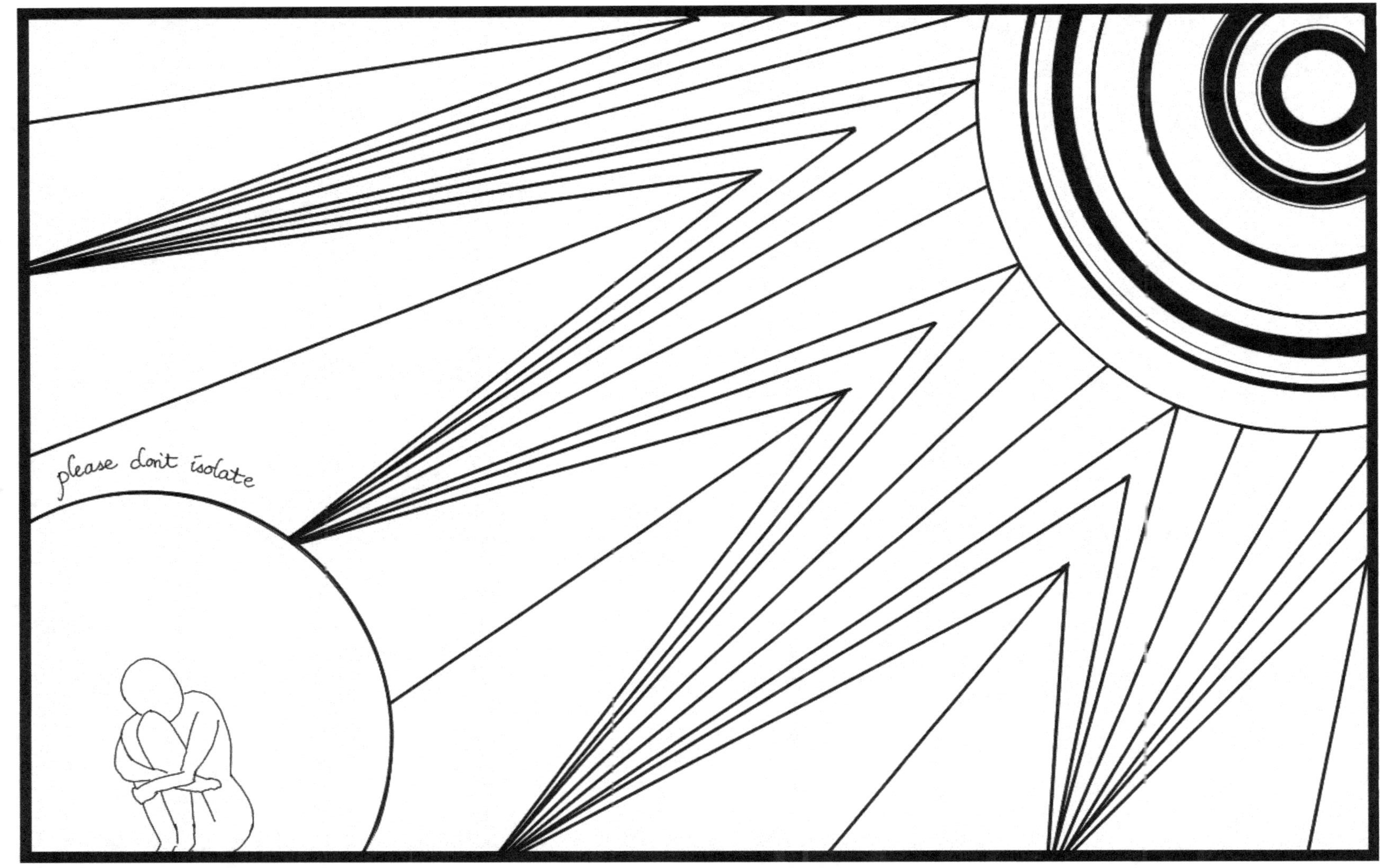

please don't isolate

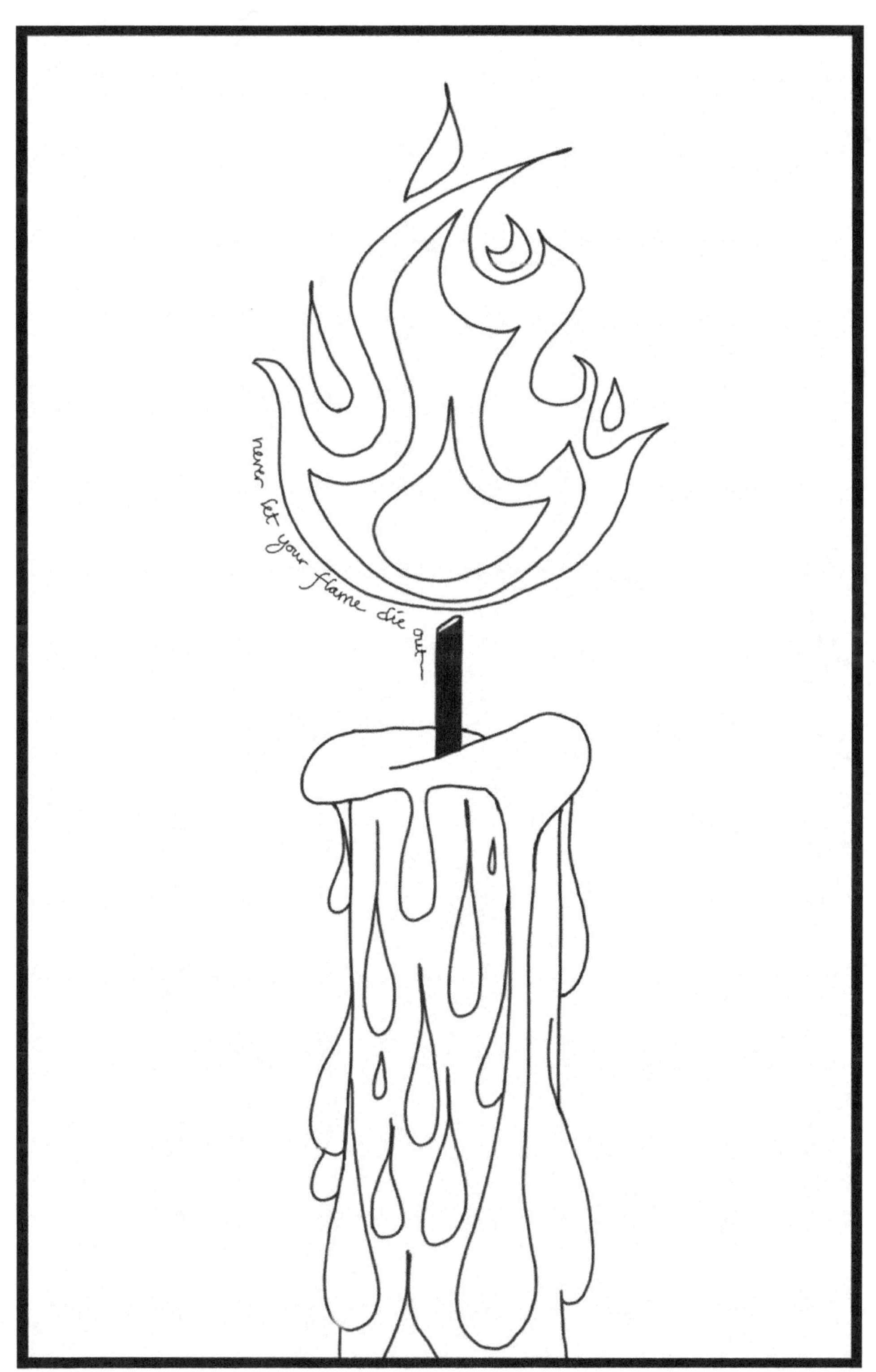
never let your flame die out

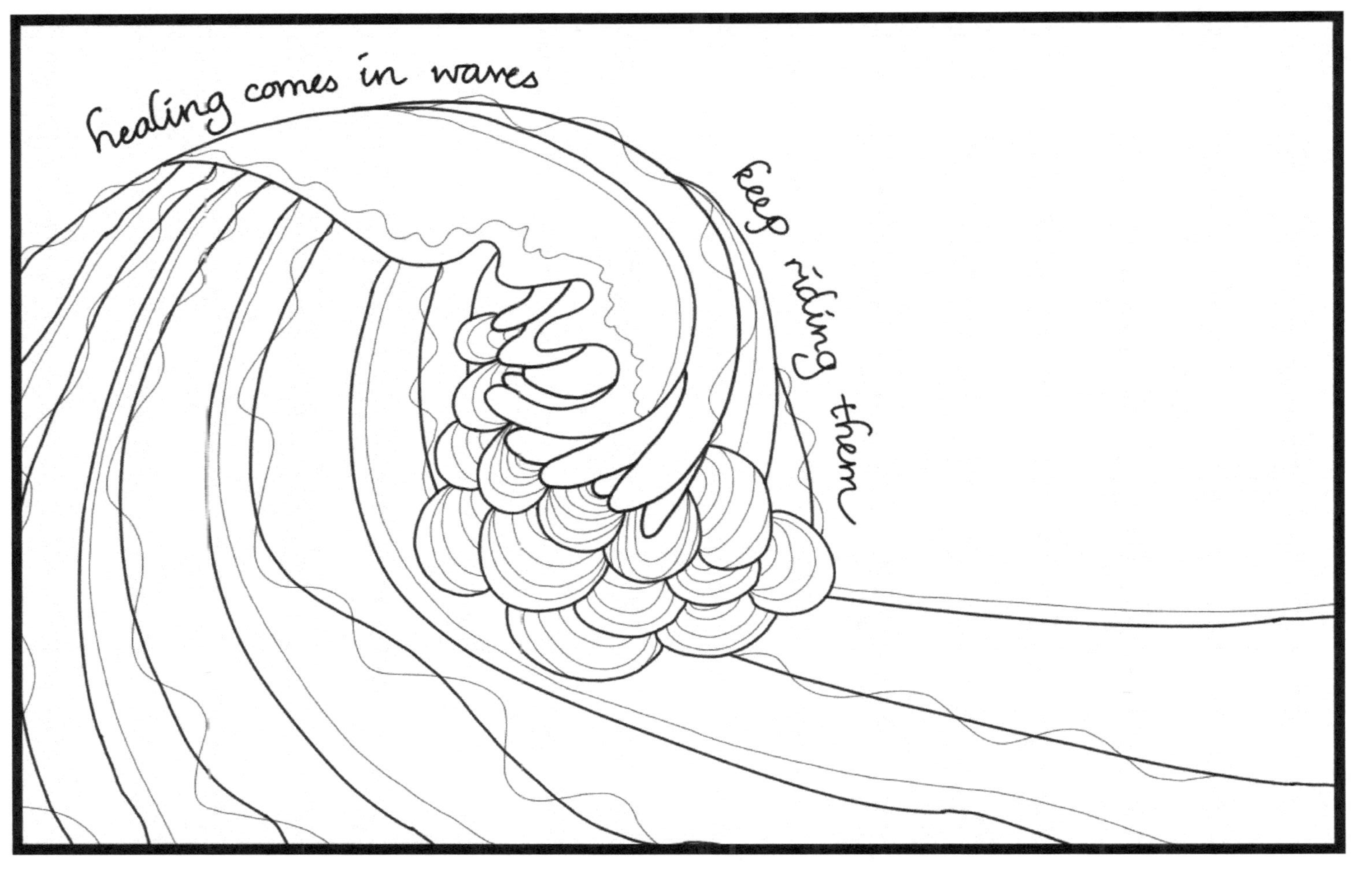
healing comes in waves
keep riding them

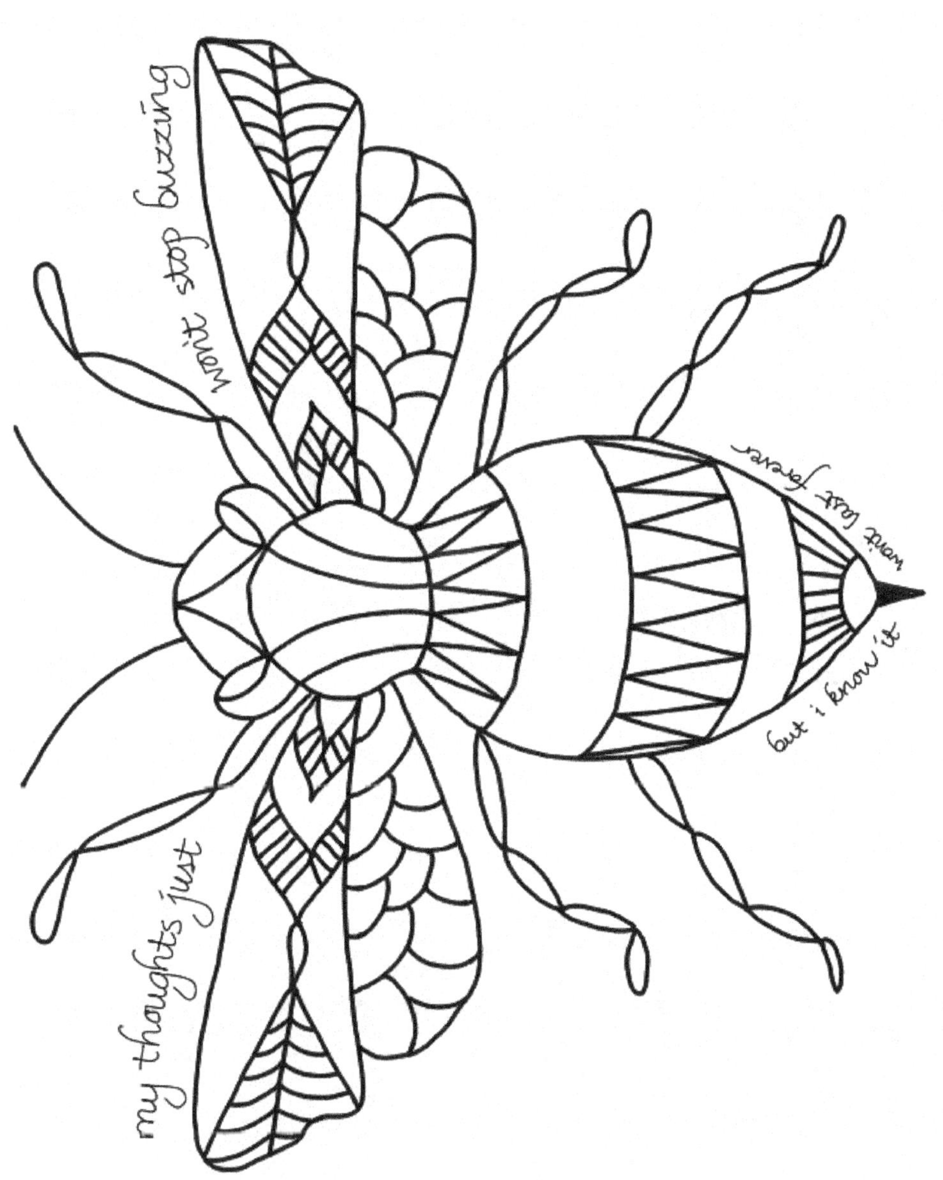
my thoughts just
wont stop buzzing
wont last forever
but i know it

some bridges should
never have been built
in the first place

draw the poison out

everyone deserves nurturing
even me
even you

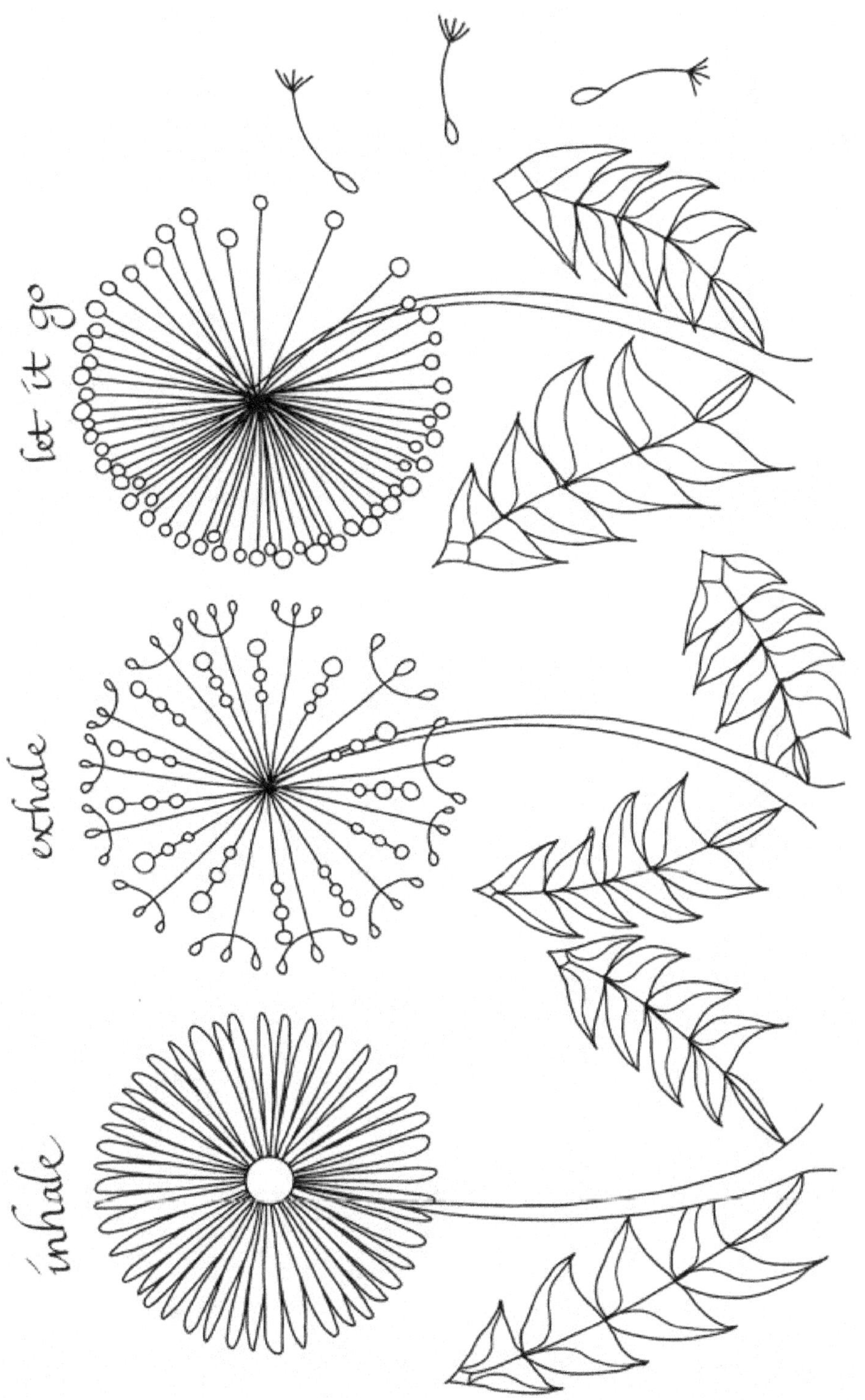

let it go
exhale
inhale

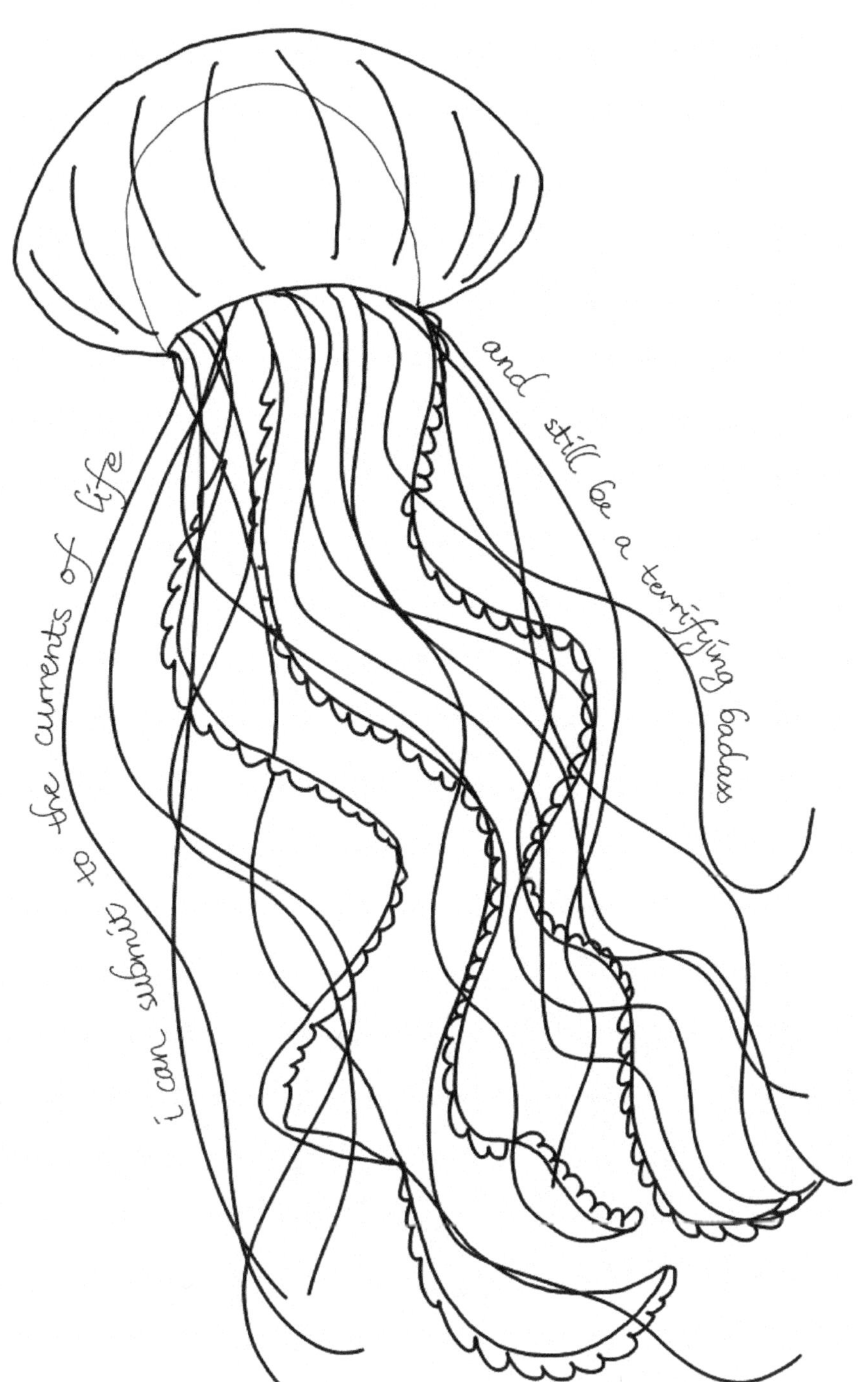

and still be a terrifying badass
the currents of life
i can swim at angles

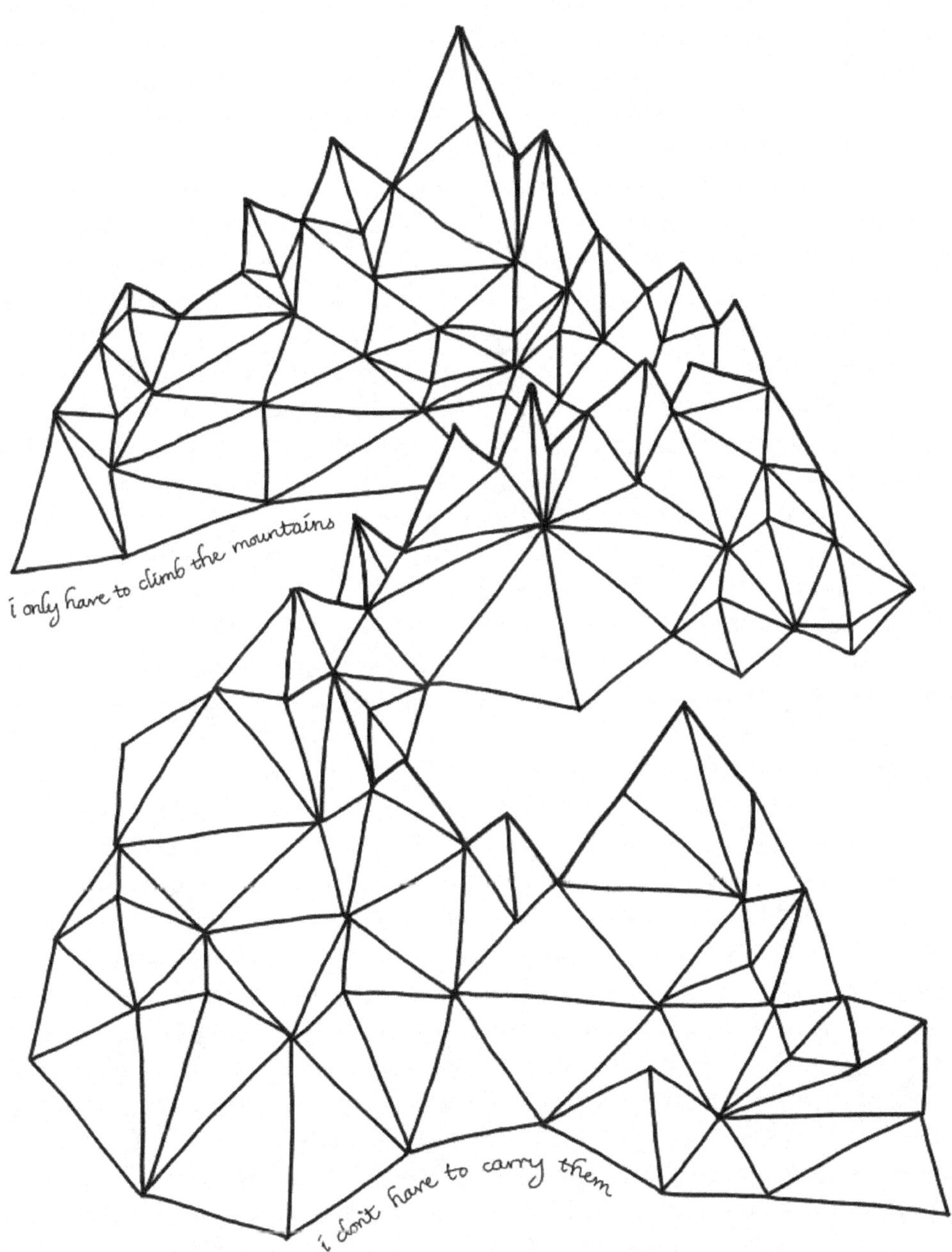

i only have to climb the mountains
i don't have to carry them

fly
even if you're afraid of falling

make your own way
N
W
E
S

the mask
take off

be kind to yourself

love yourself more

let your light shine

strut your shit unapologetically

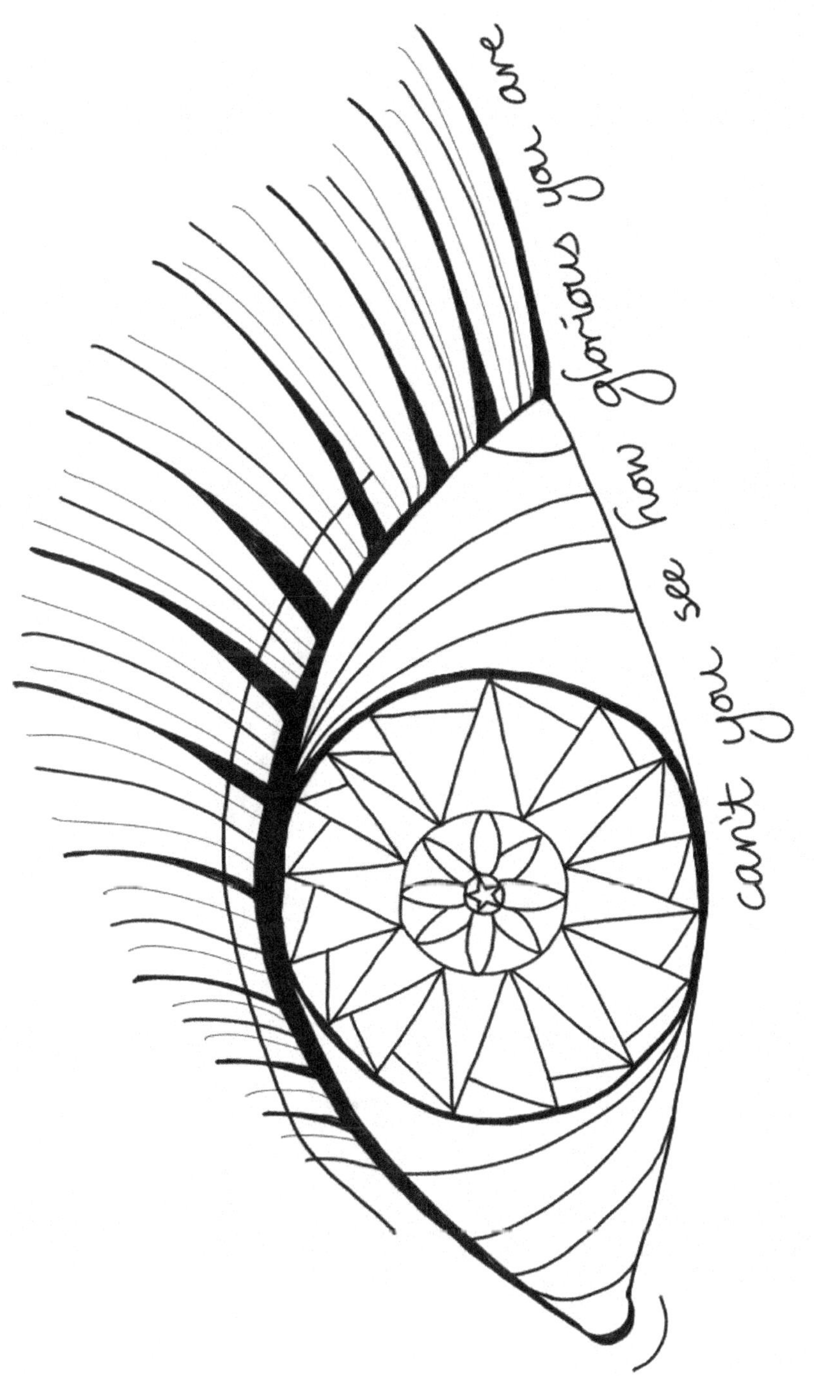
can't you see how glorious you are

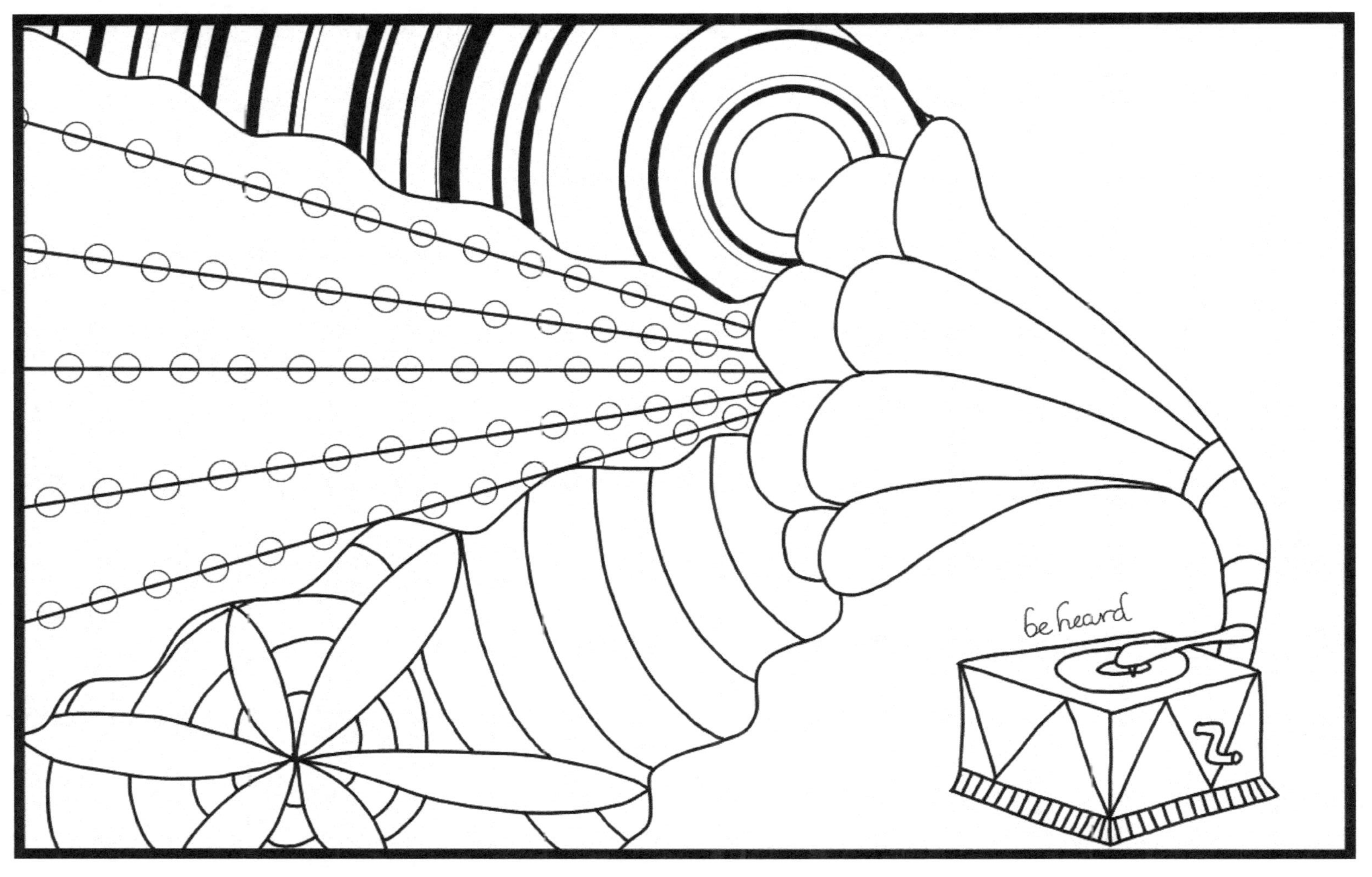

be heard

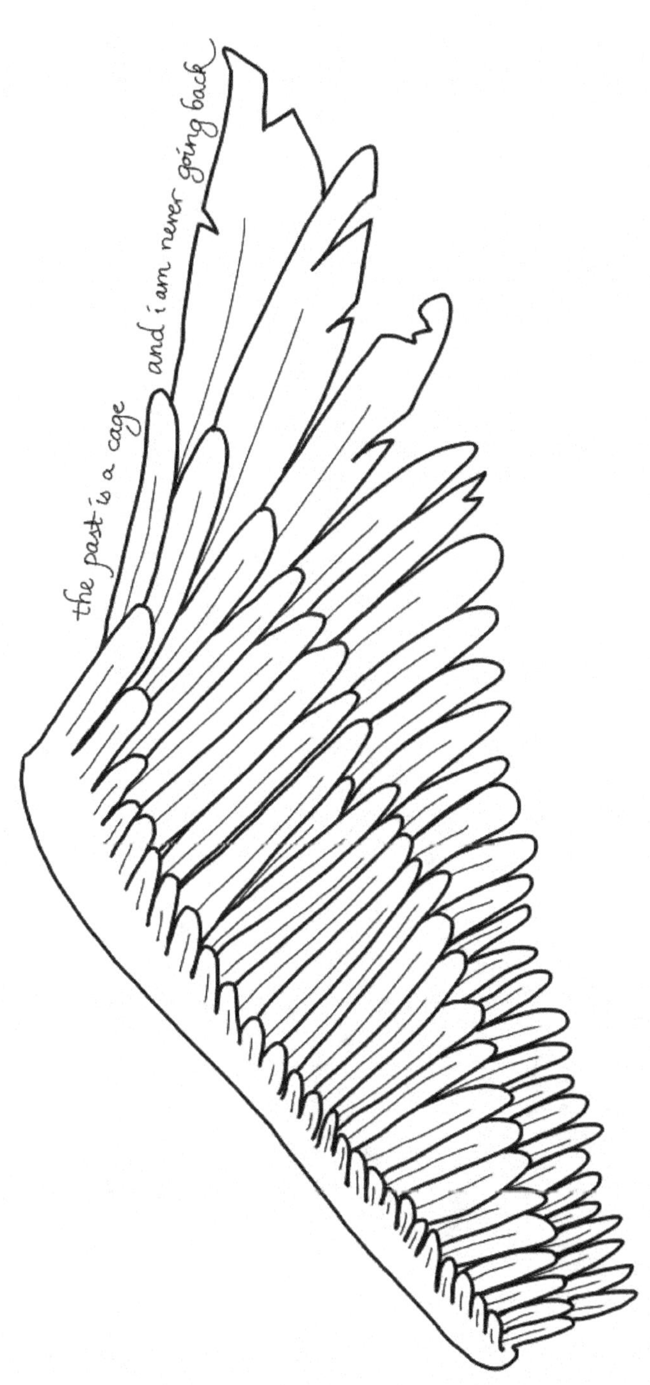

the past is a cage and i am never going back

shine like it
they say we're star dust

you made it this far
you can go a little further

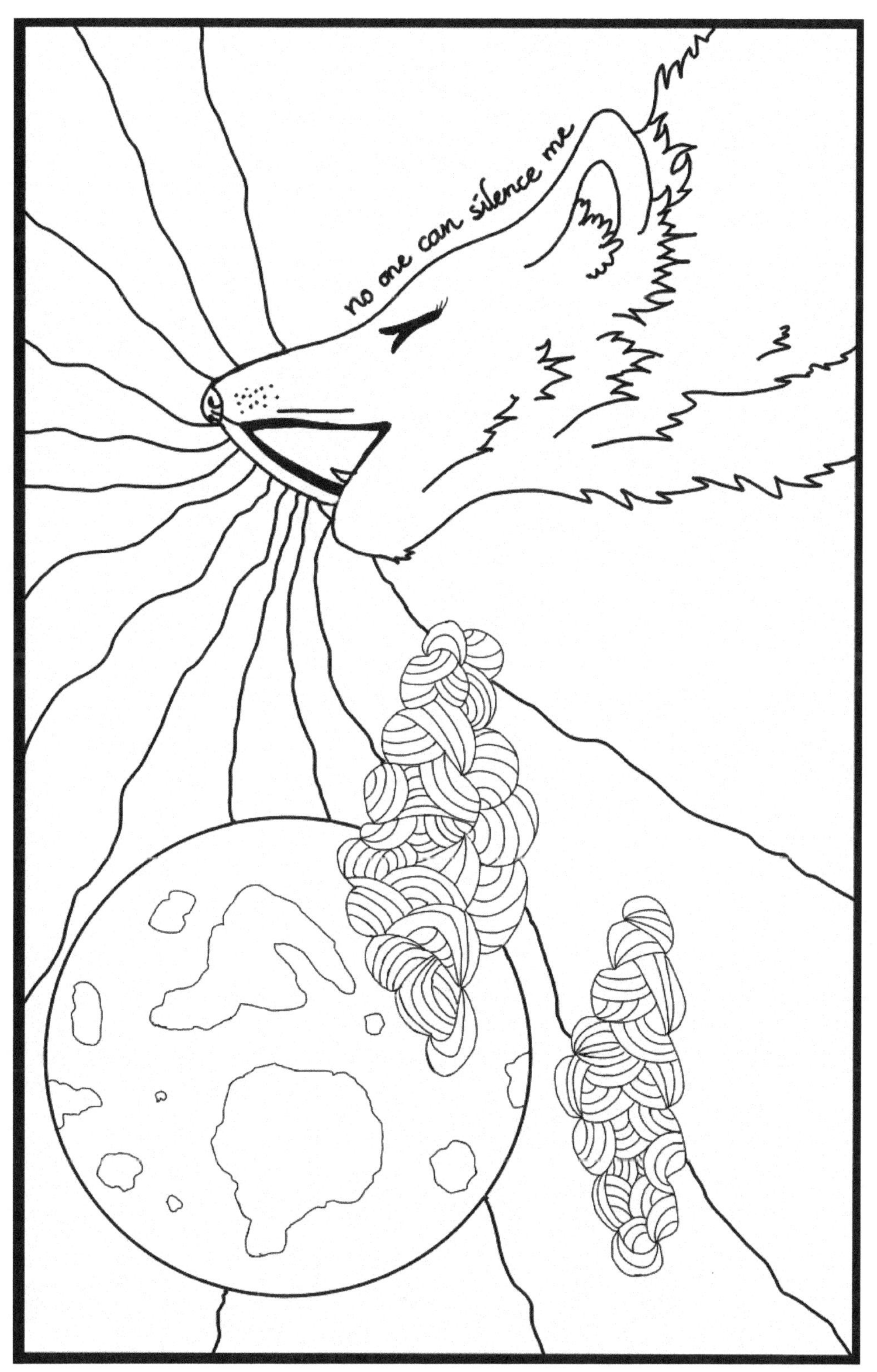

no one can silence me

everyone expects a
lotus in these things
so here

roar your truth